At a Port

by Alex Yu
illustrated by Meryl Henderson

Core Decodable 44

Mc Graw Hill Education

Bothell, WA • Chicago, IL • Columbus, OH • New York, NY

MHEonline.com

Send all inquiries to:
McGraw-Hill Education
8787 Orion Place
Columbus, OH 43240

ISBN: 978-0-02-133624-1
MHID: 0-02-133624-5

Printed in Canada.

9 10 11 12 KOD 24

A ship heads north to shore.

A ship blasts its horn.
It is in a port.

This box is for a truck.
This box is lifted out.

The trucks head out to stores.

This is a forklift.

It gets more out of the ship.

The ship sets back out.
It heads for the next port.